To children—of all ages—who appreciate the small things —R.G.

For my nephew, Anthony —A.L.

Millbrook Press™
An imprint of Lerner Publishing Group, Inc.
241 First Avenue North
Minneapolis, MN 55401 USA

For reading levels and more information, look up this title at www.lernerbooks.com.

Designed by Kimberly Morales.
Main body text set in Chaloops. Typeface provided by Chank.
The illustrations in this book were created with pencil drawings and digital coloring
in Photoshop.

Library of Congress Cataloging-in-Publication Data

Names: Gibson, Roberta Lynn, 1959- author. | Lambelet, Anne, illustrator.
Title: How to build an insect / by Roberta Gibson ; illustrated by Anne Lambelet.
Description: Minneapolis : Millbrook Press, [2021] | Audience: Ages 5–9 | Audience:
    Grades 2–3 | Summary: "Visit a whimsical workshop and follow along as we learn
    How To Build an Insect! Conversational text and playful illustrations introduce
    readers to insect body parts in this charming picture book." —Provided by publisher.
Identifiers: LCCN 2019039501 (print) | LCCN 2019039502 (ebook) |
    ISBN 9781541578111 (trade hardcover) | ISBN 9781728401478 (ebook)
Subjects: LCSH: Insects—Juvenile literature. | Handicraft—Juvenile literature.
Classification: LCC QL467.2 .G53 2021 (print) | LCC QL467.2 (ebook) |
    DDC 745.5—dc23

LC record available at https://lccn.loc.gov/2019039501
LC ebook record available at https://lccn.loc.gov/2019039502

Manufactured in the United States of America
3-53490-47792-6/6/2022

HOW TO BUILD an INSECT

Roberta Gibson

Illustrated by Anne Lambelet

Millbrook Press / Minneapolis

Let's build an insect.
Where should we start?

Humans have a head.

Most animals have a head.

Let's give our insect a head.

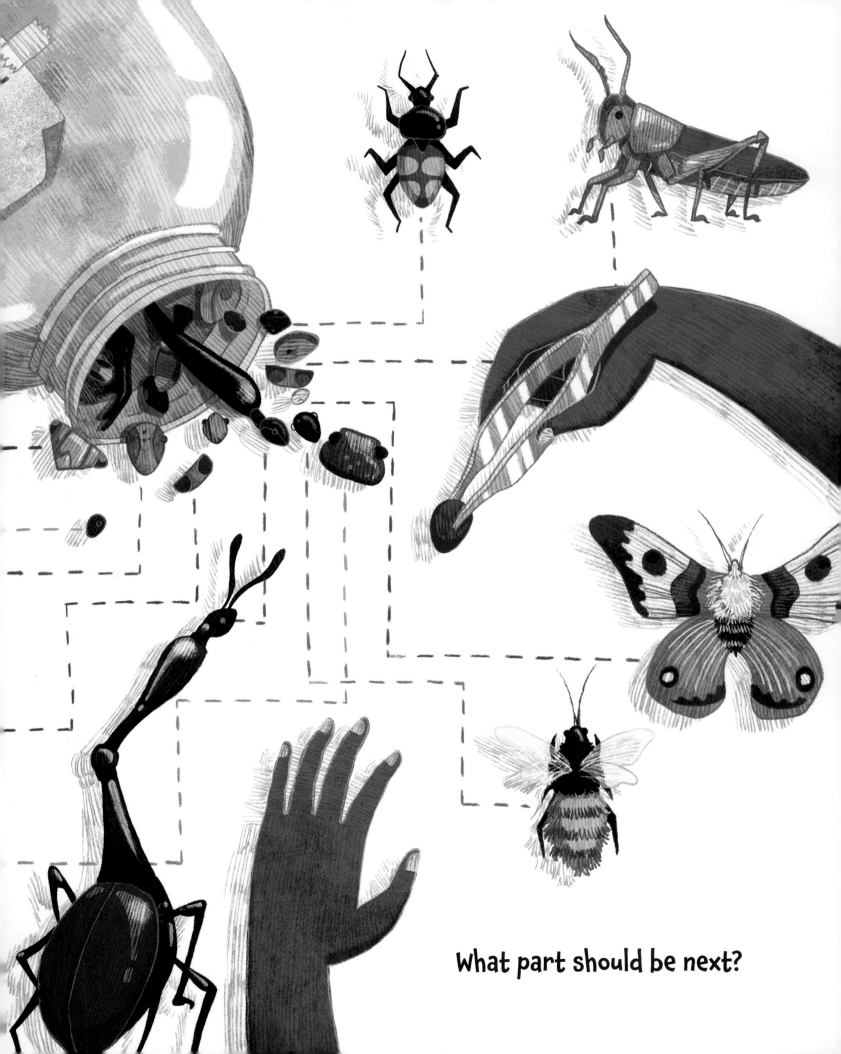

What part should be next?

Below our head, we have shoulders and a chest.

An insect's chest is called its thorax.

Let's add a thorax.

diagram 1

head

torso

What body part comes after the thorax?

We have a stomach below our chest.

An insect's stomach is in its abdomen.

← head
part 1

← thorax
part 2

abdomen
part 3

We should give our insect an abdomen.

Now it has three body parts:
head, thorax, and abdomen.
All insects have these three parts.

What else should we add?

What about bones like ours?

Should we give it a skeleton?

No. There isn't any room for big bones inside a small insect.

Exoskeletons

The Skeleton

skull

clavicle

humerus

rib cage

ulna

spine

ra

femur

phalanges

fibula

An insect has its skeleton on the outside.
It is called an exoskeleton. The exoskeleton
keeps the inside stuff in and the outside
stuff out.

tella

tibia

50 LEGS

2 LEGS

8 LEGS

How will the insect move?

Give it some legs.

How many legs?

Two like us?

Four?

Eight?

Too many. Eight legs would make it a spider. A spider might eat our insect.

AAAAaaaaah!!

I'M HUNGRY!

← 4 → LEGS

Six legs?
That is better.

6 LEGS ↙

Where do we put the legs?

Not on the head.

Put them on the thorax.

Do insects have feet?

Yes! Let's give our insect special feet so it can walk upside down.

climb, ant, climb!

Humans don't have wings, do we?

Most adult insects do have wings.

What kind should we add?

Some insects have clear wings that are easy to fold. Others have hard or leathery wings.

How many?

Attach two wings for flies and four wings for everything else.

If we give the insect two hard wings and two soft wings, we make a beetle.

Fly, beetle, fly!

How will our insect see?

Let's give it some eyes!

How many? Two?

Guess again. Five!

1

2

3

4

5

Five?

Yes, two big ones called compound eyes and three little eyes called simple eyes, or ocelli.

Peek, praying mantis, peek!

What about ears?

Some insects have flat patches in their exoskeleton that act like ears.

Where should we put them? On its head?

An insect can have its ears anywhere.

Music to my knee ears!

It can have ears on
its thorax, on its
abdomen, or even
on its knees!

Listen, cricket, listen!

An insect also needs to eat and drink.

Let's add a mouth.

Caterpillars eat leaves.

What kind of mouth would a caterpillar need?

How about a mouth like a pair of scissors to cut up its food?

Those are called mandibles.

TASTE

Chomp, caterpillar, chomp!

TACKS

If butterflies sip sweet nectar, what sort of mouth would they need?

How about a straw?

A butterfly's mouth is a curled straw. It is called a proboscis.

Sip, butterfly, sip!

How will our insect smell and touch things?

2 antennae

4 antennae

Put on some feelers called antennae.

How many? Four?

Four would make it a shrimp or lobster.

Those are not insects, are they?

Let's give it two antennae.

Where?

On the head!

Extra feelers on the abdomen are called cerci.

Cockroaches and crickets have cerci.

HELP ME!

antennae

cerci

What else does an insect need?

How about a way to breathe?

Should we give it lungs?

GASP

Lungs will not work
because the exoskeleton
can't move in and out.

What can we do?

Put holes in the sides
of the body.

Call them spiracles.
They let air into and out
of the insect's body.

air out

air in

Now we can decorate our insect. Add:

hair...

or horns...

or spikes:

These things disguise the insect from predators and protect it from harm.

Are we done?

No, not quite . . .

Let's give our insect a place to live and a snack.

or Spots.

Now we're done.
Good job!

MORE ABOUT INSECT BODY PARTS

Eyes

Insect vision is different from ours. Insects have compound eyes made up of many individual units called ommatidia, each covered with a lens called a facet. Because of how they are built, compound eyes are good at detecting movement.

Insects like dragonflies have large compound eyes that take up much of their head. In contrast, some insects are blind or have only a few ommatidia.

Certain insects can see color. For example, honeybees can see the colors of the rainbow except red, and they can see a color we can't called ultraviolet. Honeybees can also see a color known as "bee's purple," which is a mixture of yellow and ultraviolet.

Mouthparts

The mouthparts of insects are quite complex. Insects with chewing mouthparts, like beetles, caterpillars, dragonflies, and grasshoppers, have mandibles that move side to side like shears. In addition, they have a second set of chewing surfaces right under the mandibles called maxilla. Insects that chew also have an upper lip, or labrum, and a lower lip called a labium. Attached to the maxilla and labium are fingerlike structures called palps that taste and move around the food.

Adult butterflies and moths may have a tube for a mouth, called a proboscis.

True bugs, like box-elder bugs or shield bugs, have piercing-sucking mouthparts. Within the proboscis are thin blades called stylets that can cut into plants or other insects. Once the stylets pierce the food, the insects can suck up the liquids inside.

A housefly has a sponge for a mouth, which it uses to drink liquids. If a housefly finds something solid to eat, like sugar, it spits saliva on the food to make it liquid before it drinks it.

Ears

Some insects can detect sounds. Singing insects like cicadas, crickets, and katydids can sense vibrations using a patch of flexible membrane called a tympanum. The tympanum acts like the head of a drum.

Spiracles

The spiracles in the insect's thorax and abdomen open into a series of tubes called tracheae. Oxygen in the air goes into the insect and travels down to the cells. The same tubes carry carbon dioxide, a waste product, out of the insect.

Abdomen

The word *abdomen* comes from a Latin word that means "belly." Inside the insect's abdomen are the organs for digestion, excretion, and reproduction.

Wings

Having wings is a special trait. Only a few different kinds of living animals have wings: birds, bats, and adult insects.

Insect wings come in all shapes and sizes. Cockroaches or grasshoppers have wings that are leathery. Bees, wasps, dragonflies, and mayflies have flexible membranous wings. True bugs, like box-elder bugs or milkweed bugs, have wings that are leathery halfway down and membranous at the end. Beetles have hard upper wings called elytra. Hidden under the elytra are membranous wings that fold up. Beetles raise the elytra and move the under wings to fly. Finally, butterflies and moths have four big wings covered with colorful scales.

Legs

Insect legs can be divided into five sections. The coxa and trochanter are sockets that connect the leg to the insect's thorax. The femur is like our thigh, the tibia is similar to our lower leg, and the tarsus is a group of segments (tarsomeres) that form the insect's foot.

The legs are not all identical. For example, praying mantises have enlarged front legs for grasping prey. Honeybees have curved surfaces on their back legs called pollen baskets for carrying pollen.

Thorax

The word *thorax* comes from a Greek word that means "chest." The thorax of insects is divided into three segments: the prothorax is closest to the head, the mesothorax is in the middle, and metathorax is closest to the abdomen.

GLOSSARY

abdomen: the third or hind body section of an insect

antennae: a pair of organs on an insect's head that sense the environment. Different parts of the antennae can sense smell, touch, and even sound in some insects. Just one is an antenna.

cerci: a pair of organs on the end of the abdomen of insects like crickets and cockroaches that is used to sense danger coming from behind the insect

exoskeleton: the outside covering of an insect's body

mandibles: jaws located on either side of the head that act like a pair of scissors

ocelli: tiny simple eyes used mostly to detect light. Just one is called an ocellus.

proboscis: a long, slender tongue that acts as a straw to bring the liquids (nectar and water) to the insect's mouth

spiracles: openings in an insect's exoskeleton that allow air to pass inside the body

thorax: the thorax is the middle part of the insect between the head and abdomen. It is the anchor point for six legs as well as wings in the adults.

STEAM ACTIVITY: BUILD AN INSECT MODEL

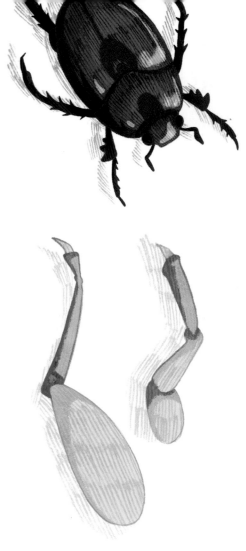

1. **Gather the following materials:**
   - white computer paper (for wings)
   - construction paper (for body parts, antennae, and legs)
   - glue sticks or tape
   - crayons, colored pencils, markers, or a combination of these
   - age-appropriate cutting implement, such as safety scissors

   Optional materials (as available and age appropriate):
   - chenille stems
   - egg cartons
   - seeds
   - sheet protectors or wax paper (for wings)
   - colored tissue paper
   - pom-poms
   - Styrofoam balls
   - sponges

2. **Using the text for instructions and illustrations for inspiration, build your own insect model.**

3. **Using scissors and construction paper, carefully cut out circles and ovals for your insect's head, thorax, and abdomen. Cut strips of paper to use as legs and antennae.**

4. **Decorate your insect using the materials you have gathered.**

5. **Put your insect on display!**